FOOTBALL

RYAN JAMES

Rourke
Educational Media

rourkeeducationalmedia.com

*Scan for Related Titles
and Teacher Resources*

TABLE OF CONTENTS

GET PSYCHED!

Hut one! Hut two! Hike! You race down the football field holding the ball to your chest. You spin around a linebacker trying to stop you.

You leap into the end zone.
Touchdown! You celebrate
with your teammates. You are
psyched to play football!

A football field is simple. It is a large rectangle with two smaller rectangles. The smaller rectangles are the end zones.

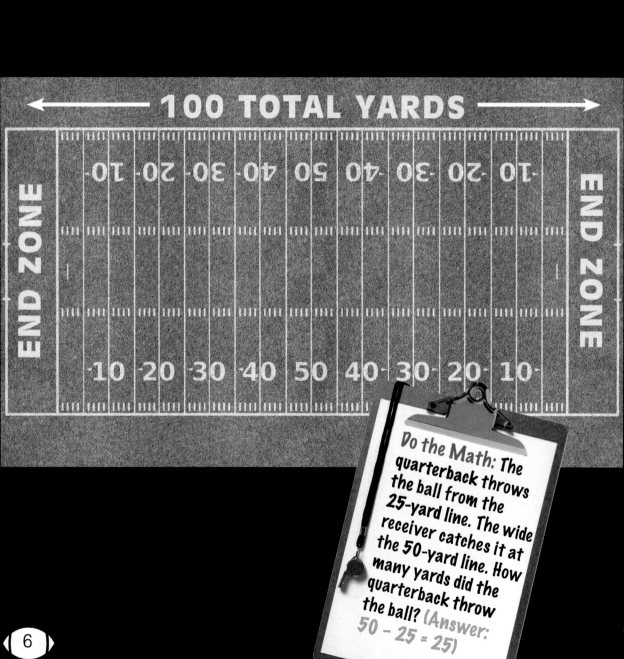

100 TOTAL YARDS

END ZONE

-10 -20 -30 -40 50 40- 30- 20- 10-

-10 20 30 40 50 40 30 20 10-

END ZONE

Do the Math: The quarterback throws the ball from the 25-yard line. The wide receiver catches it at the 50-yard line. How many yards did the quarterback throw the ball? (Answer: 50 – 25 = 25)

The field has many white lines. The hash marks, or short lines, show the yards. There are also numbers at the 10, 20, 30, 40, and 50 yard lines.

GAME ON!

The offense needs to move the ball ten yards in four plays, called downs. If they are unable to score or move the ball forward the ten yards, the other team gets the ball at the line of scrimmage. Then the play changes direction.

The distance between each hash mark is one yard.

GAME ON

Football is a popular team sport in the United States. It is played by people of all ages.

Football is a tough sport with eleven players on each team going head to head. While the team on offense has the football they attempt to score. Players on the defense try to stop the offense from scoring by tackling other players or blocking the ball.

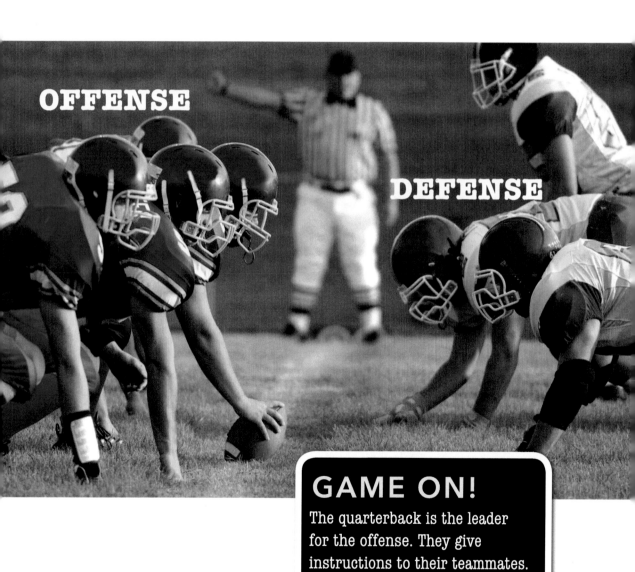

OFFENSE

DEFENSE

GAME ON!

The quarterback is the leader for the offense. They give instructions to their teammates.

To score points, players on the offense carry or kick a football into the end zone. A touchdown is six points. The team can then try to kick through the goal post for one extra point or run the ball into the end zone again for two points. A field goal is worth three points.

3 WAYS TO SCORE POINTS:

Catching the ball in the end zone.

Running the ball into the end zone.

Kicking the ball through the goal posts.

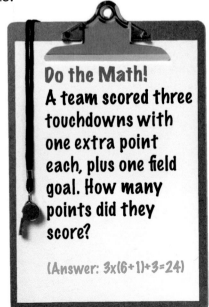

Do the Math!
A team scored three touchdowns with one extra point each, plus one field goal. How many points did they score?

(Answer: 3x(6+1)+3=24)

Every player on both teams has an assigned position. Some positions require size and strength while others require speed and agility.

OFFENSE

Lineman – Protects the quarterback.

Quarterback – Typically the team's leader. This player controls if the ball is handed off to the running back or thrown to a receiver.

Running back – This player gets the ball if the team chooses to run with the ball instead of throwing it. They are also eligible as a receiver if they do not hand the ball off.

Receivers – These players run "routes" and try to fool their defender. The quarterback tries to throw them the ball if they can get free from their defender.

DEFENSE

Lineman – Tries to tackle the opposing quarterback or running back.

Linebackers – They help the backs on a pass play or the lineman on a running play.

Defensive Backs – Safeties and corner backs usually line up with the receivers to try to prevent the quarterback from throwing to them. If they catch the ball, it's called an interception.

SPECIAL TEAMS

Kickers – These players punt the ball after the offense is stopped, and kick the ball off to the other team after scoring.

Snappers – Snap the ball to the quarterback or the kicker.

Returners – These players catch and return the ball to score touchdowns.

Tacklers – These players tackle the returners.

SUIT UP!

Football players wear jerseys with numbers on the back. This makes them easier to identify, since everyone looks the same in their uniforms and helmets. It also lets scorekeepers track player's stats, such as rushing yards, points, and tackles.

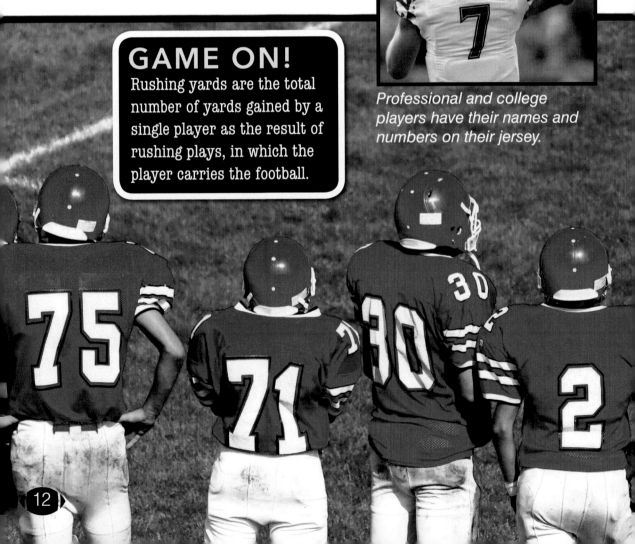

GAME ON!

Rushing yards are the total number of yards gained by a single player as the result of rushing plays, in which the player carries the football.

Professional and college players have their names and numbers on their jersey.

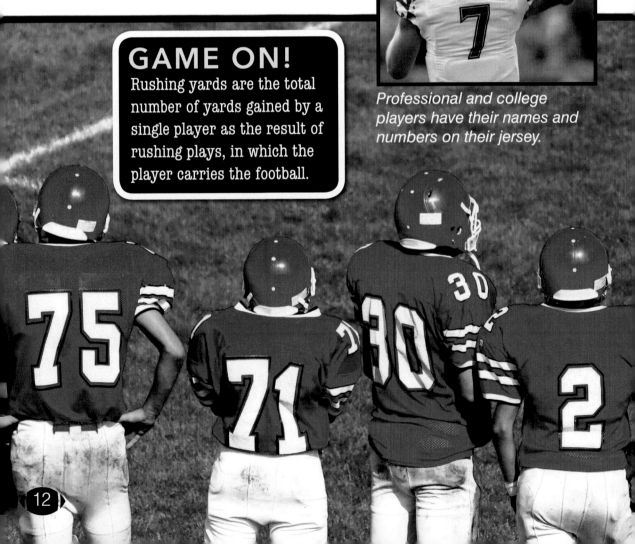

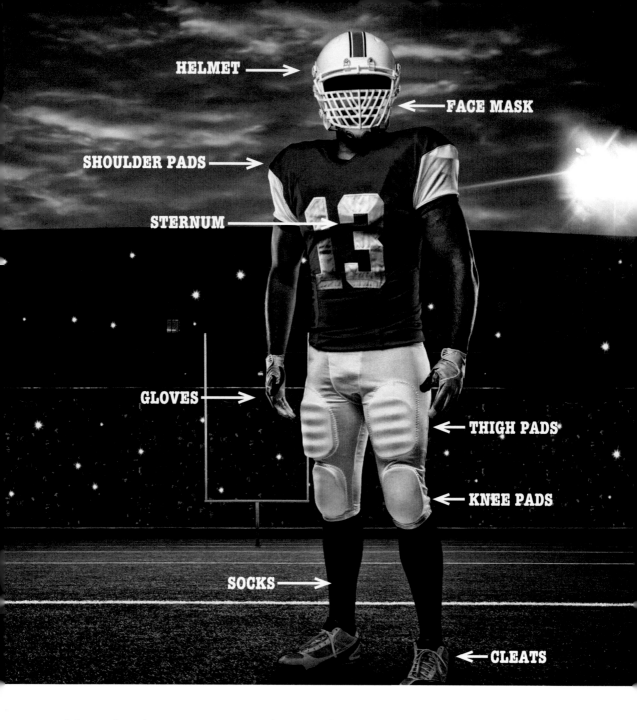

HELMET ⟶

⟵ FACE MASK

SHOULDER PADS ⟶

STERNUM ⟶

GLOVES ⟶

⟵ THIGH PADS

⟵ KNEE PADS

SOCKS ⟶

⟵ CLEATS

You don't want to get hurt when you get tackled. So a player wears shoulder pads under his or her jersey. They also wear pads to protect their arms, legs, and **sternum**.

You don't want to slip on the field. Players wear cleats for **traction**. The cleats help the shoes dig into the turf.

Football is a rough game. Players wear helmets and face masks to prevent them from getting hurt. A mouth guard keeps the player's teeth and tongue safe.

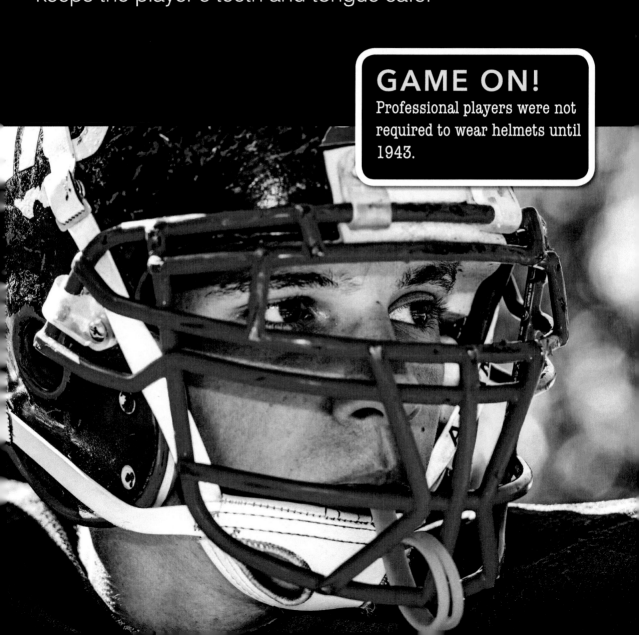

GAME ON!
Professional players were not required to wear helmets until 1943.

THROUGH THE YEARS

The first football game was played between two colleges. It happened on November 6, 1869, in New Jersey. The rules were based on rugby.

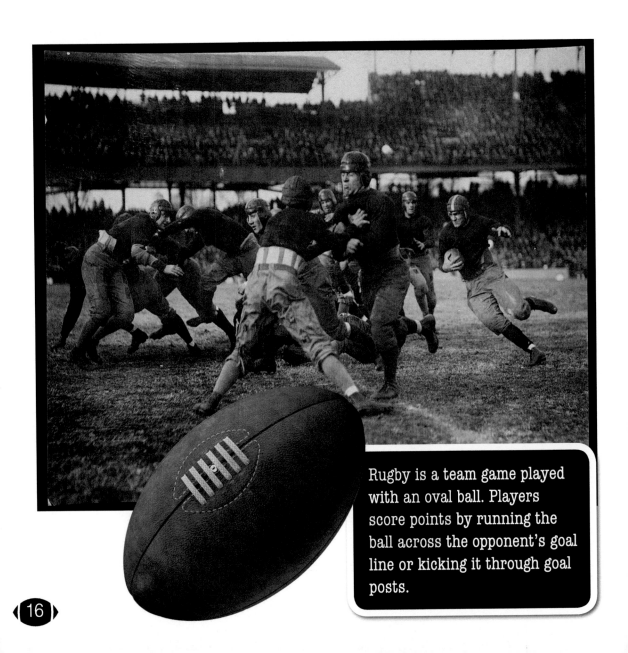

Rugby is a team game played with an oval ball. Players score points by running the ball across the opponent's goal line or kicking it through goal posts.

While he was a football player at Yale from 1876 to 1881, Walter Camp changed the rules into what is now the **modern** game of football.

*Walter Camp
1859–1925*

EVOLUTION OF THE GAME

Walter made changes to the rules every year from 1876 to 1880. He also added new rules. He became a member of the Intercollegiate Football Association in 1880. The association began using Walter's rules that year.

The Outing, *published in November 1895, had articles written by Walter Camp, known as the Father of American Football.*

The National Football League (NFL) started as the American Professional Football Association. The **inaugural** season was in 1920 with teams from Ohio.

Do the Math: How many years later was the first NFL game played after the first college football game? (Answer: 1920 – 1869 = 51 years)

In 1920, the Decatur Staleys, also known as the Staley Starch Makers, were a team in the American Professional Football Association. They later became the Chicago Bears.

The NFL now has 32 teams in many U.S. states. Both the American Football Conference and the National Football Conference each have 16 teams. The conferences are broken up into 4 divisions; East, North, South, and West.

	AFC	NFC
East	■	●
North	■	●
South	■	●
West	□	○

GAME ON!

Canada has its own professional football organization called the Canadian Football League (CFL). It has nine teams.

SCIENCE OF FOOTBALL

There's a science to this game! A quarterback uses **physics** when throwing a ball. He will throw harder if the receiver is farther away.

The angle of a punter's kick affects how far the ball will travel. When the ball leaves the punter's foot, the power used to kick the ball determines how high and fast the ball will travel.

Linebackers are coached to tackle a runner near the belly button or the body's **center of mass**. This requires less strength to push the runner down.

Computers are used to **analyze** players' moves and speed. Coaches use this information to help with training and as a strategy tool when playing an opposing team.

Scientists are making helmets safer. They are inventing special materials to decrease the risk of **concussions**, or head and neck injuries.

With players getting stronger and bigger all the time, the risk for injury increases. Scientists are always looking for better and safer ways to improve equipment.

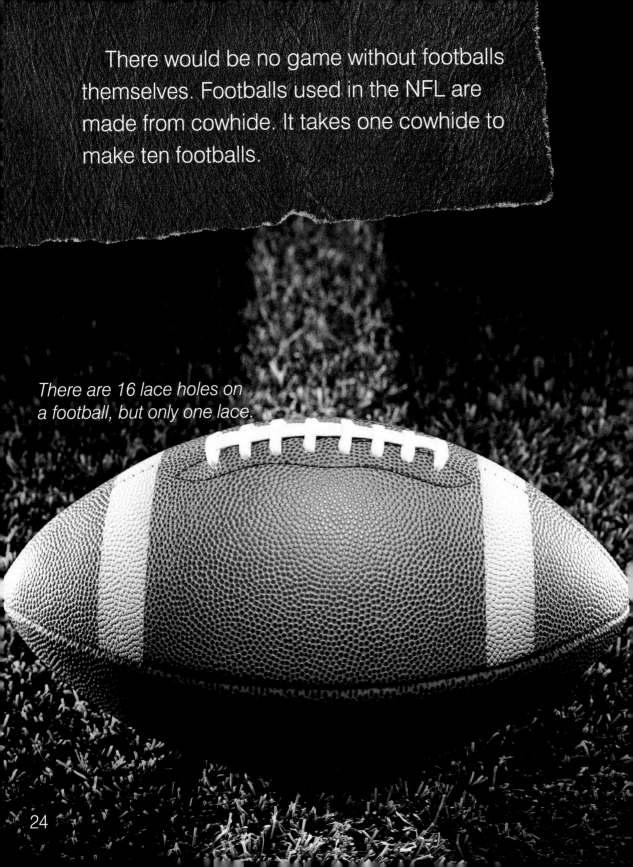

There would be no game without footballs themselves. Footballs used in the NFL are made from cowhide. It takes one cowhide to make ten footballs.

There are 16 lace holes on a football, but only one lace.

Wilson has been the exclusive maker of NFL footballs since 1941. The company produces about 4,000 balls per day.

Only the most skilled craftsmen are allowed to make NFL game balls. Only two Wilson employees on the 130-person assembly staff create NFL balls.

HIGH STANDARDS

Wilson employees can only make NFL footballs if they have at least 20 years of experience. That's some serious dedication to the game!

BEING A PROFESSIONAL

Football players have to do many things to be successful. Training every day, both on and off the field, is a must! Listening to their coaches helps them to become better, more successful players.

Coach's notes:
- Arrive at practice on time
- Eat a healthy meal before practice
- Get enough sleep
- Do your best on and off the field
- Respect everyone

Football players need lots of fluids to stay **hydrated**. Drinks that are plentiful in electrolytes help replenish what their bodies lose during a game. They also need high-calorie, healthy foods. Many eat more than the average three meals a day!

Football players are often looked at as role models. This means they need to show good sportsmanship both on and off the field.

GLOSSARY

analyze (AH-nuh-lyez): to study something in a careful way

center of mass (sehn-ter uhv mahs): the center of gravity of an object

concussions (kuhn-CUH-shuns): injuries to the brain caused by a hard collision

hydrated (HYE-dray-tihd): having the proper amount of water in the body

inaugural (in-AW-guh-rul): first

modern (MOD-urn): of today

physics (FIH-zihks): the scientific study of matter and energy

sternum (STUR-nuhm): the breastbone

traction (TRAHK-shun): grip of an object to a surface

INDEX

SHOW WHAT YOU KNOW

1. What is the job of the defense?
2. Who developed the modern game of football?
3. How is physics important in football?
4. What other country also has a professional football league?
5. Why is it important to listen to the coach's advice?

WEBSITES TO VISIT

www.science360.gov/series/science-nfl-football

www.nflrush.com

www.livestrong.com/article/16370-exercises-youth-football-workout

ABOUT THE AUTHOR

Ryan James has always loved sports. When he is not playing sports, he can be found investigating and researching almost anything. He lives in the mountains of North Carolina with his dog Bentleigh, who is always ready to catch a ball. Mr. James's favorite football teams are the Carolina Panthers and the Clemson University Tigers.

Meet The Author!
www.meetREMauthors.com

www.rourkeeducationalmedia.com

PHOTO CREDITS: Cover: ©AKsonov; table of contents, 4, 5: ©skynesher; 6: ©Pongphan Ruengchai; 7: ©Mark Herreid, ©AspenPhoto (inset); 8: ©STILLFX, ©3bugsmam, ©Nickp37; 9: ©groveb; 10: ©stevecolorimages, ©Matthisas Drobeck, ©filo; 12: ©surpasspro, ©AspenPhoto (inset); 13: ©Beto Chagas; 14: ©Perytskyy, ©AspenPhoto; 15: ©Zwawol; 16, 17, 18: Library of Congress; 17, 19: Wikipedia; 20, 22: ©AspenPhoto; 21: ©Jerry Sharp; 23: ©SCIENCE PICTURE CO/ SCIENCE PHOTO LIBRARY; 24: ©Nic_Taylor (inset), ©skodonnell; 25: ©JIM WEST/SCIENCE PHOTO LIBRARY; 26: ©pixelheadphoto; 27: ©lutherhill; 28: ©gchutka; 29: ©Steve Debenport; 30: ©Rob Mattingley

Edited by: Keli Sipperley

Cover and interior design by: Rhea Magaro

Library of Congress PCN Data

Football / Ryan James
(Game On! Psyched For Sports)
ISBN (hard cover)(alk. paper) 978-1-68191-752-8
ISBN (soft cover) 978-1-68191-853-2
ISBN (e-Book) 978-1-68191-943-0
Library of Congress Control Number: 2016932714

Also Available as:

ROURKE'S
e-Books